SHIVA SUTRA

AN EMPIRICAL STUDY – VOLUME-I
(SAMBHAVOPAYA)

ABHIJIT SARMA BORDOLOI

Contents

Contents

Dedications

Dedicated to Kāshi Vishwanāth and Mahābhairab

Right after I finished translating the Shiva Sutra, I got an unplanned opportunity to visit the temple of Shiva known as Kāshi Vishwanāth in Varanasi, which is the oldest city in the world and has been a home for scholars. It is one of the Jyotirlingas out of the twelve of them that are situated in India and Nepal. I had never visited any other Jyotirlingas before. Due to a long queue at the temple compound, it generally takes hours to have a darshan of the Shiva linga, however, on that day it took me less than half an hour, even after paid Sugam passes were closed for the day. I was able to have an easy darshan and touched the Jyotirlinga. I felt blessed! I took this as a sign from the universe that I was on the right path and I should proceed with writing a complete book and publish it.

The temple of Mahābhairab has always been in my heart of hearts, because I have visited this temple since my childhood. My grandmother was very fond of going to this temple and I used to visit with her mostly. Bhairava, who is an incarnation of Shiva, is the main archetype that has been mentioned in the Shiva Sutra. Bhairava also holds a lot of significance in Kashmiri Shaivism. That is why I want to dedicate this book to Mahābhairab as well.

Preface

As perplexing as it may sound, one day while praying to mother goddess Lakshmi, I received a divine inspiration to translate the Shiva Sutra of Vasugupta. Even more perplexing was the fact that I was praying with the hymn called Kanakadhārā Stotram composed by Adi Shankarāchārya, who is known to have had some sort of rivalry with the Shaivism tradition of Kashmir to which the Shiva Sutra is said to belong. Translating a Sutra text is not new for me though, as for the last several years I have been independently researching on the Yoga Sutra of Patanjali. I have already translated all of the Yoga Sutra and extracted all its secrets. I am writing a complete book on the Yoga Sutra as well, which is likely to take a few years to complete. I read the Shiva Sutra a few years back from multiple free documents that I downloaded from the internet, so I already knew that this scripture exists. The inspiration that I mentioned above renewed my interest in the Shiva Sutra. The online versions that I got to read were almost identical and mostly done like academic research. I came across some published books on the Shiva Sutra, but I did not purchase any of those books. I want to confess that I have not even read the Spanda Kārikā, which is the original commentary composed by Vasugupta himself, who "discovered" the Shiva Sutra. Because of the inspiration that I mentioned previously, I wanted to try translating the Shiva Sutra myself with a fresh perspective based on modern science, spirituality and my existing research on the Yoga Sutra. If there are similarities with other published books, it is purely coincidental. If any other author has had a similar revelation as mine, we both would obviously arrive at a similar conclusion. Shiva is a master of Yoga as well as Tantra. Both disciplines though different have many similarities. My research has been based on Yoga. However, my native place (Assam) is known as the birthplace of Tantra. There is Tantra in its air, metaphorically speaking. So, I suppose I do have a kind of birthright to work with Tantra. Regarding the Shiva Sutra in particular, I have found that the teachings are a mix of Yoga and Tantra. It has been an exciting and enlightening journey to find the meaning of its verses. I am hopeful that the readers will also experience the same.

Introduction

The Shiva Sutra is a scripture which contains the process that a spiritual seeker can follow to transform oneself from an ordinary mortal to an enlightened individual. Enlightenment to me is the realisation of our true self as a divine light. This light is self-illuminating which gets hidden in the thickness of the material world. As a result of divine inspiration, many people in the past had awakened this light in them. There are many among us who also have awakened. It is the duty of the awakened ones to help the seekers to rekindle this light in them. When we have a manual like the Shiva Sutra, it becomes a lot easier to transform ourselves to become the light beings that can bring more peace and harmony to the troubled humanity.

Vasugupta was a sage in Kashmiri Shaivism tradition. He is known to have brought the scripture Shiva Sutra to that tradition. According to legend, Vasugupta did not himself compose the Shiva Sutra, but he found it inscribed on a rock which was revealed to him by Shiva himself in a dream. So, we don't really know exactly how old the Shiva Sutra is. It may have been inscribed on that rock thousands of years ago. Vasugupta wrote the book Spanda Kārikā as a commentary on the Shiva Sutra. So, this leaves an open space for any devotee of Shiva to write their commentary on the Shiva Sutra based on their unique understanding of the scripture. There have been many commentaries done on the Shiva Sutra by other authors. My translation of the Shiva Sutra is primarily based on my independent research on the Yoga Sutra of Patanjali.

This translation is not a word by word translation. I try to understand the meaning of the whole verse and then write down the meaning that comes up from my Pratyaya (a type of intuition) in English. The meanings that I have arrived at have caused positive transformations in my life. Therefore, I feel motivated to share these revelations in the form of a book. I have named this book as Shiva Sutra - an Empirical Study. The word Empirical has two meanings. One of the meanings is "evidence based". I have tried to incorporate as much relevant scientific information as I could gather and tried to explain in terms of such research backed data. The other meaning of the word empirical is "experience based". Whatever explanation I have given in this book is based on my personal experience. I have not partnered with any other practitioner or author while writing this book. Since I do not hold relevant academic credentials, I have written this book as a student, so I am calling it a Study.

I am not an authority in science, Yoga or Tantra. I have been working in an engineering profession, so I know how to fit things together and make things functional. My career has also taught me how to build and innovate. I am definitely not writing a textbook; rather this book should be treated as a presentation. I am showcasing a new horizon of possibility to understand this scripture.

I have had a deep interest in Spirituality since childhood. I feel privileged and grateful now that I have been able to write a spiritual book on my own. Shiva Sutra teaches us how to be deeply spiritual. The word Sutra can be translated as "hint". These types of scriptures give hints about certain spiritual teachings.

The scripture Shiva Sutra has three chapters, which contain three methods. These three methods are for attaining liberation from limiting perceptions. Each of these three methods is enough unto itself. Whoever has understood and practiced any of these methods can attain liberation from limiting perceptions. In this Volume-I of my book, I have explained the first method Sāmbhavopāya - the Whole Self method. I have already translated all of the Shiva Sutra in my own style, and am working on explaining Volume II and III in the form of books. I am hopeful to publish books on the other two methods within a year. The way I have written my book on Shiva Sutra is a blending of spirituality, religion, science and motivational content.

There are two ways to live our life. Either we live a focussed life or a distracted life. The four basic human goals are Dharma, Artha, Kāma and Moksha. It may sound like these goals need to be achieved in a serial manner; however, we can also strive for these goals in parallel. Even if it is not mentioned clearly in this scripture, I have understood that Shiva Sutra teaches how to achieve these goals simultaneously. In fact, after we realise our true potential, it becomes much easier to achieve our goals.

I will be also making references to another scripture that comes from Kashmiri Shaivism, which is called the Vigyana Bhairava Tantra (VBT in short). The VBT is a scripture that contains about 112 meditation techniques. I have practiced several of these meditation techniques for a few years and with which now I feel so much spontaneity that I don't have to practice them voluntarily anymore. The significance of the VBT scripture is that it helps one to have spiritual achievements while engaging in worldly duties, without living an ascetic lifestyle.

Kashmir is called the Heaven on Earth due to its unparalleled beauty. Kashmir has also been one of the most favoured places for mystics of the ages, as it has a natural mystical environment. There is even a story about Jesus Christ travelling to and living in Kashmir after his resurrection. Kashmir was originally named after the sage Kashyap who belonged to the time when the Vedas were composed. I feel that one of reasons why I received inspiration from goddess Lakshmi to translate the Shiva Sutra is because Kashmir is also known as the abode of goddess Lakshmi. Infact, the name of the capital city of Kashmir is Srinagar. Sri or Shree is one of the names of goddess Lakshmi, so Srinagar means City of Lakshmi. Mother Lakshmi is the goddess of wealth. Wealth means not only riches. Having peace of mind is also a kind of wealth. Being someone of influence is also wealth. Health is ofcourse wealth. Abundance and well-being are the features of wealth.

Kashmiri Shaivism was the predominant sect of Hinduism in Kashmir for a long period of time starting from around 850 AD. It is a tradition mainly based on Tantra. Many tantric systems such Trika and Srividya originated in Kashmir. The Shiva Sutra is said to belong to a non-dualistic branch of Kashmiri Shaivism. The followers of the Kashmiri Shaivism tradition got scattered all over India and around the world due to political conflict which resulted in their eviction from Kashmir, similar to the way the Tibetans had to flee after their homeland was forcefully occupied by another country.

Among all the mystics and sages of the Shaivism tradition of Kashmir, Abhinavagupta is the most well known. Abhinavagupta was a figure of great genius and talent. He created a great number of compositions, such as, scriptures, poems, music, dance forms etc. Due to his genius, Kashmiri Shaivism reached its peak during his lifetime. He created a long lasting tradition of illustrious disciples who created their own compositions. Abhinavagupta was born in a Kanyākubja Brāhmin family of scholars and mystics whose ancestors were originally from Kannauj, Uttar Pradesh. There is a legend in our family and relatives which states that our ancestors were also Kanyākubja Brāhmin who immigrated to Assam on request of the king of Kāmrūp (old name of Assam). Sometimes it makes me wonder whether we belong to the same bloodline. But this is just a butterfly in my stomach, so please don't take the previous sentence literally.

Modern Science though has made great progress; if we compare it with ancient knowledge then science is still like a teenager who is studying in a high school and is yet to study in college and university. What I mean to say is that Modern Science has achieved great milestones; however, it may want to recognise that there are also a great number of milestones which the ancients had already accomplished. It may seem like in today's world only science is making progress. But if we look closely we will see that the world of spirituality is also progressing equally. There are a few relatively new branches of science, such as Quantum Physics and Epigenetics, which are in alignment with ancient teachings like Yoga and Tantra.

In my book I will be using the phrase Whole Self (or simply Self), which is known as Brahman in Advaita Vedānta. In the Yoga Sutra of Patanjali the Self is called Drashtā (seer). The common word in Sanskrit for the Self is Paramātmā, which means Supreme Self. I like to use the phrase Whole Self because, as we will learn from the Shiva Sutra, the Self is not only the Supreme, but also the gross. The gross or mundane is the foundation of the Supreme. Patanjali also says that one Guna is born from another. Transformation is the nature of Samsāra. Whatever transformation happens, it happens within the Whole Self. So, from an overall perspective we can say that the Whole Self is unchanging. The following Vedic Hymn illustrates the same:

OM, pūrnamadah pūrnamidam pūrnāt pūrnamudachyate
Pūrnasya pūrnamādāya pūrnamevāvaśiśyate

The external world is Whole. The Internal world is Whole. The Whole manifests from the Whole. When the Whole is separated from Whole, it is still Whole.

CHAPTER ONE

WHO IS SHIVA?

Karpoora Gauram, Karunā Avatāram, Samsāra Sāram...

One whose glow is as white and purifying as camphor, One who is the incarnation of benevolence, One who is the essence of the world...

The meaning of Shiva is genuine goodness or benevolence. Shiva is known as the most benevolent of all the deities in Hinduism. Shiva's appearance is that of an introverted alpha-male. He has a third-eye that represents omniscience. Rest of his appearance can give shivers to any simpleton. In spite of his chilling appearance, Shiva is the most straightforward of all. Shiva is associated to the element of Earth. In fact, he is so earthly that he is actually said to be living on earth, on top of a mountain peak called Kailāsha in the Himalayan mountain range. His source of power is his calmness. His calmness is so profound that he rides on the back of a great ox named Nandi, and it does not protest.

Shiva is also commonly known as Shankar. To me Shankar

is one who never judges. Shiva is said to treat gods, demons, mortals or immortals alike. He is ready to bless anyone who has been able to witness him.

Shiva is also called Mahādeva. The word Deva can be loosely translated as Lord. In Hinduism we have the concept of lords for every aspect of the world. There is a lord of water, lord of fire, lord of Sun, lord of moon, lord of each planet, lord of heaven, even lord of machines, and so on. Mahādeva means lord of the lords. So, Shiva is like a permanent president of the universe, hence he is called Mahādeva.

Howsoever we may interpret Shiva, fundamentally he is the purest essence. Each and every one of us is a spark of this essence. His spark exists in all of us. The Shiva Sutra is one of the ways to rekindle the spark within us. Once we realise Shiva's essence, we can feel our oneness with infinity.

CHAPTER TWO

THE METHOD

Sāmbhavopāya

The Whole Self Method

The title of the first method has the name of Shiva as Shambhu. I believe that the name Shambhu means - the timeless lord of the universe. What we call "time" is simply a measurement of duration. In reality, time is something insubstantial. If we chant Shambhu Shambhu, it gives a feeling of timelessness. To Shiva, past and future are illusions (Māyā), because the only time that exists is the present moment.

There are two similar sounding names of Shiva, which are Sāmba and Shambhu (also pronounced Sambhu). The name Sāmba symbolizes Shiva and Shakti together. Since this method in Shiva Sutra is mainly dedicated to Shiva, so I believe the name Shambhu is more appropriate. The words Bhava or Bhu mean world, earth or universe. Anyhow, since both the names belong to the same deity Shiva, so the confusion does not matter.

Another word that sounds plausible is Sambhava, which means possibility. It may be relevant too, because if we can properly learn the teachings in Sāmbhavopāya, we can make what seems impossible to be possible. Towards the end of this book, I will explain a Yogic principle called Samyama, which I like to translate as "sameness". The word Sambhava can be broken down as Sam-bhava, which means - the feeling of sameness with the universe. By using the powerful principle of Samyama, even something seemingly impossible can be made possible.

There is another name of Shiva that is mentioned in this method is Bhairava. According to the Vigyana Bhairava Tantra (VBT), Bhairava represents fullness or wholeness. There are many Dhāranās mentioned in the VBT, which we can practice to call on the fullness of Bhairava. A Dhāranā is an active-imagination. It is the opposite of Vikalpa which is passive-imagination that is akin to daydreaming, commonly known as mind wandering or internal chatter. While assuming a Dhāranā we direct our awareness to the goal of realizing fullness. Although Bhairava is generally worshipped in several forms as a warrior idol, in VBT he is practiced as formless. We may call him Mahā Bhairava. In my native town, there is a temple Mahābhairab which is said to have existed since the Dwāpara Yuga, i.e. more than 5800 years ago. In this temple there is no idol of Bhairava, but a huge Shiva Linga is worshipped. Shiva Linga was once a universal symbol of Yin-Yang energy. There was a time when it was used all over the world. Archaeologists keep finding Shiva Linga like structures during excavations even in distant countries. Nowadays, the worship of Shiva Linga is mostly confined to Hinduism.

The Shiva Linga at Mahābhairab is said to be swayambu, which means self-emanating. It is said that the presence of this Shiva Linga was revealed to a king in his dream, who was able to find it and then built a temple around it. There are many such swayambu Shiva Lingas in India. The worship of a Shiva Linga can clear the effect of negative thought-forms from a large area. The real meaning of the structure of a Shiva Linga is a mystery, surrounded by many theories. There are also many types of Shiva Linga and each has its own significance.

CHAPTER THREE

VERSE 1-1

caitanyamātmā

Undifferentiated Consciousness is the Self.

Consciousness, in general, is considered to be intangible. Spiritualists however believe, and many have seen what is known as the Divine White Light. This light is our highest reality, which is all pervasive. We, as well as the universe are an expression of this light. In the Yoga Sutra this light is called Pratibhā (Prati-ābhā), meaning all pervasive light. Only someone who has been able to open their Crown Chakra (Sahasrāra) can see this light. I use a method from the Yoga Sutra called Mūrdhajyoti to open my own Crown Chakra. Once it opens, my head gets filled with this light, so much so that it seems like my head has disappeared and only the light exists. I even watch my chest and bones becoming filled and glowing with this light. It is a very soothing experience though, I love it! I have realised that once we have connected to this light via the Crown Chakra, we can also connect to it by other means such as mantra chanting.

White light contains all spectrums of light. If we pass a beam of white light through a glass prism, the refracted light shows all the colour spectrums. So, white light is basically an undifferentiated light. Just like the white light that we see physically, the Divine White Light also contains all spectrums and is undifferentiated. Each Chakra in the system of Kundalini has an associated colour. As the Divine White Light reaches the Chakras it gets differentiated into the particular colour associated with a Chakra. It works just like the glass prism.

This Divine White Light is our true Self, which is the self of all and the universal Self. As one is able to elevate one's consciousness, it gets more and more filled with this light, ultimately realising that there is no difference between one's own consciousness and the all pervasive Divine White Light.

Currently there is no scientific instrument that can directly measure the Divine White Light. However, brain scans of advanced meditation masters have repeatedly revealed that many regions in their brain glow during meditation. During the well known Double-slit experiment also it was proven that human observation altered the behaviour of light particles called Photons. In this experiment when the scientists observed the light, it behaved like the light consisted of photon particles, however, when the light was not being observed by the scientists, it behaved as if it was a wave. So, the consciousness of the observers altered the behaviour of light. Therefore, we can infer that consciousness and light are interrelated. It may even be that light (even tangible light) and consciousness is both one and the same thing!

CHAPTER FOUR

VERSE 1-2

jñānambandhah

Knowledge of the world is what confines the Whole Self.

Knowledge is simply perceptions stored in memory. If we consider an object, such as a piece of string, we call it so because that is what we perceive it to be. If we break it down then we will see that the piece of string is made of plastic fibre or organic material such as jute. That material consists of molecules. Then molecules consist of atoms, which consist of electrons, protons and neutrons. Probably even these smallest particles can be broken down further. So, we have perceived the object to be a piece of string for our own convenience. There is no end to how we can perceive something. The perceptions get stored in our memory which is what we call knowledge.

The mind appears to exist only because of its activities. Otherwise the mind is like still water, transparent. The ripples and waves make the water appear to exist. So is the case with the mind. Different perceptions cause ripples in the mind that makes it appear to exist.

Due to different perspectives there appear to be limitations in the world. Usually the human mind remains clouded by such apparent limitations. However, the universe does not believe in limitations. When we reach a universal perspective, we can see that the limitations that we believe in are only apparently so.

Memory contains all the impressions of the past. Fundamentally, these impressions are of pain or pleasure. What is in our memory is considered to be the known territory. Anything outside this is the unknown territory and considered, in general, as unsafe. Memory also contains information about the people that are considered friends and foes. These memories are important to an extent that we need to be aware of dangers.

Memory also contains our identity and habits, which tend to determine our decisions. Our identity can contain limiting patterns that were impressed on memory in the past. The identity determines what type of habits we grow. Therefore, our worldly identity is not who we truly are. Actually, we are the all-pervasive consciousness.

VERSE 1-3

yonivargakalāśarīram

Energy of different densities interacts with cosmic light of higher frequencies to create/ transform matter.

The tradition of Tantra is known for its use of secrecy. It uses symbols and metaphors to encrypt the actual meaning. Even if this verse is written in plain Sanskrit, if we take the literal meaning, that may not be the right conclusion.
The literal meaning of the word Yoni is the groin area of the human body. But that is just a surface level understanding. What is behind the surface is known as the lower dantian in Chinese healing systems. The lower dantian is said to be the storehouse of energy in the human body. In Sanskrit the name for the lower dantian is Brahmā Granthi. Brahmā is the Creator aspect of the almighty. Thus it signifies that the Yoni area is filled with creative energy. The horizontal part of a Shiva Linga is called the Yoni and it represents Shakti (liberated energy). In a human body the Yoni area is situated near the Swādhishthāna Chakra. Swa means own

and Adhishthāna means residence. Swādhishthāna is the original place of the dynamic Kundalini energy, because it means "own residence". As I have shown several reasons above, due to which we can now conclude that in this verse, the word Yoni is synonymous with Energy.

There is another meaning of the word Yoni which means "species". But I do not see any clear reason why it should be relevant with this verse. I had to choose between the two meanings, so I chose the former one because it is going to be more relevant.

We can take the literal meaning of Vargah as Classification. Energy may be classified depending on its density. The scientific definition of Energy Density: It is defined as the amount of energy stored in a given system or a region of space per unit volume. Energy density = Energy stored / volume.

There is in fact a classification of Energy Density in Tantra as well, which is classified as Aghora, Ghora and Mahāghora. These correspond to the three Gunas - Sattva, Rajas and Tamas respectively.

The word Kalā means cosmic light beams. It is the cosmic light that is received on earth from the Sun, Moon, stars and planets. In astrology it is believed that the placements of the planets in a birth-chart determines the course of a person's life, and can even shape the history of a country. Astrology is legally recognised as a science in India. The phases of the Moon determine the tidal current of the oceans. The light of the Sun evaporates surface water to form clouds. In many known and unknown ways the celestial bodies impact the activities on earth.

In Quantum Physics, matter is considered to be composed of particles as well as waves. If we consider the inside of an atom, most of it is empty space in which smaller particles such as electrons are floating. The tangibility of matter emerges due to interactions among quantum fields that surround the particles. Thus, in quantum physics, the behaviour of matter is very different from its behaviour that is described by classical physics. Mass corresponds to matter, because only matter can have mass.

In this verse we have three components:

1. Yonivarga - densities of energy

2. kalā - light beams

3. śarīram - body or matter (mass)

Let us represent #1 with E, #2 with c and #3 with m. We can use them as the following variations of Albert Einstein's equation for mass-energy equivalence relationship:

Einstein's equation:

$$E = mc^2$$

Variations:

$$E/c^2 = m \quad \text{or} \quad m = E/c^2$$

If c represents the speed or frequency of ordinary Light. then c^2 may represent light of a higher frequency.

I want to make a hypothesis about the meaning of this verse as follows - Energy of different densities interacts with cosmic light of higher frequencies to create/transform matter.

I may not have been able to mathematically pinpoint this formula like a physicist or mathematician. My purpose is to simply show how closely this verse in Shiva Sutra resonates with the formula for mass-energy equivalence relationship derived by Albert Einstein.

CHAPTER SIX

VERSE 1-4

jñānādhisthānamātrikā

Knowledge resides at the level of consciousness.

I have contemplated several possible meanings of the word Mātrikā and I found the most relevant meaning to be a scale. It is a scale for measuring levels of human consciousness. The word Mātrikā may have been derived from the word Mātrā, which means level. In Shiva Sutra, three levels of consciousness are mentioned which are waking level, dreaming level and deep sleep level. Modern neuroscience also measures consciousness with machines such as Electroencephalogram (EEG) that reads the brainwave frequencies. The types of brainwave frequencies are named as Gamma, Beta, Alpha, Theta and Delta.

- Gamma is a very high frequency that is similar to a fight or flight response. It measures between 25 and 100 Hz.
- Beta is the frequency of the ordinary waking consciousness. It measures between 12 and 30 Hz.

- Alpha frequency is of dreams and daydreaming. It measures between 8 and 12 Hz.
- Theta is the frequency that is found at the threshold of falling asleep. It measures between 4 and 8 Hz.
- Delta is the frequency of dreamless deep sleep. It measures between 0.5 and 4 Hz.

These frequencies keep circulating from one to another depending on the type of activity a person is involved in. Through the practice of meditation it is possible to voluntarily shift from one frequency to another. The lower frequencies which are Alpha, Theta and Delta have remarkable problem solving and healing potential. If we reach Alpha frequency during meditation, we can recall long forgotten memories. At Theta frequency it is possible to alter deep seated beliefs. If one can reach Delta frequency then it is possible to even remember past lives. Thus at such lower frequencies we can gain access to knowledge that is not ordinarily available.

VERSE 1-5

udyamobhairavah

Call on Bhairava to rise.

As discussed previously, Bhairava represents the consciousness of the Whole Self. This is a consciousness that is free from fears and limitations. There are meditation techniques given in VBT that can raise our consciousness from the three lower Chakras to the higher Chakras. The three lower Chakras are Mulādhāra, Swādhishthāna and Manipura. These three Chakras contain the limiting patterns of instinct, desire and ego respectively. By practicing the Dhāranās given in VBT we can raise our consciousness to the Heart Chakra or higher. The Heart Chakra is known as Anāhata, which literally means unstruck. Basically, Anāhata implies non-reactivity or Wu-Wei. Once consciousness is concentrated on the Heart Chakra, there is an effortless relaxation of the mind. Opening of the Heart Chakra brings positive emotions of gratitude, fulfilment and kindness. Raising our consciousness brings us closer to the wholeness of Bhairava and we feel that nothing is lacking.

When consciousness is raised to the Third-eye (Agya) Chakra, it is possible to feel a sense of omnipresence. We realize that we are the infinite intelligence that exists everywhere in the universe. This feeling of infinity is very liberating. The word Agya means to allow or order. In the Chinese esoteric book Secret of the Golden Flower, the third-eye is called the holy king, to which everything else obeys. When we focus attention on the third-eye chakra, which is located at the centre of the forehead, any disturbances in the subconscious mind can be calmed down and controlled. I have experienced that paying attention to our breath can assist in focussing consciousness in the third-eye. Meditating on the third-eye relaxes the mind and we are able to access deeper layers of our existence.

CHAPTER EIGHT

VERSE 1-6

śakticakrasandhāneviśvasamhārah

Bhairava finds one's energy channels to bring an end to the worldly identity.

Every human being is a miniature universe. The macrocosm has a corresponding aspect in the microcosm that is the human body. For example, the index finger is associated with the planet Jupiter and it also corresponds to the element of Air. In several Yoga scriptures it is mentioned that there are about 72,000 Nādis or energy channels in a human body. There are three central energy channels called Idā, Pingalā and Suśumnā. These three correspond to Moon, Sun and Fire respectively. According to Advaita Vedānta, the Brahman constitutes everything. It has constituted everything in the universe and our world. I like to think of Brahman as the "original element".

By raising our consciousness through the Chakras, we align more and more with the consciousness of the universe itself. At one point we realise that we ourselves are the universe. This is the realisation called Aham Brahmāsmi. The universe has manifested itself in the form of a human being on earth. We are not just a limited identity that is bound to a human form. Universal consciousness is that of omnipresence. It is all over the place and it is also the place. The worldly personal identity that we developed through sense perceptions gets superseded by a universal identity called Bhairava.

CHAPTER NINE

VERSE 1-7

jāgratsvapnasusuptabhede
turyābhogasambhavah

One can experience the Turyā state while waking, dreaming and in deep sleep.

Turyā is a meditative state also known as Samādhi. There are two types of Samādhi: Sabeeja (with seed) and Nirbeeja (without seed). The "seed" here refers to our identity. In the Yoga Sutra, Samādhi is defined as a state where there is an utter absence of a self-image. As a result of the rising of Bhairava consciousness, our worldly identity is superseded and that is how we can reach the state of Samādhi or Turyā. When there is no self-image then everything seems like one whole. There are no real boundaries in this state. This is Oneness. All is One!

In Samādhi state the activities of the subconscious mind are minimized. In general, our subconscious mind tries to "control" our life, but it makes choices based on only what it has known and experienced in the past, mostly from external sources. So, the range of its thinking is limited. Due to this a lot of decisions that our subconscious mind makes turn out to be wrong. In Samādhi state, we realise that we do not have to control our life. Life balances itself on its own. When we relax into our own being we activate higher faculties of intelligence, such as conscience and intuition. These faculties help us to make much better decisions.

In this verse, the three levels of human consciousness are mentioned - waking level, dreaming level and deep sleep level. Turyā literally means "the fourth". So, Turyā or Oneness is the fourth level of consciousness. We need to practice Oneness during meditation and wakefulness, and then gradually we can start feeling Oneness during dreaming and deep sleep as well.

CHAPTER TEN

VERSE 1-8

jñānamjāgrat

Waking level is where one is actively participating with knowledge.

During the waking hours our brainwave frequency is mostly at Beta level. Whenever, we are engaged in any activity or conversation, our brainwave frequency remains at Beta. Sometimes while daydreaming we also reach the Alpha frequency. Whatever activity we engage in while awake, involves active participation with knowledge. The Conscious mind which is known as *mann* in Sanskrit is active during the waking hours. Conscious mind however occupies only 10 percent of all brain activity. Remaining 90 percent activity is from the subconscious mind.

Due to the voluntary nature of the Conscious mind, we can have thoughts and emotions of our own choosing. Thus it is during waking hours that we can realise Oneness more easily through practices such as meditation.

Mindfulness is a practice of Buddhist origin which focuses on disciplining the conscious mind, while we are awake. In this practice one has to be fully present and focussed in the present moment, being aware of one's thoughts and feelings without judging. This also involves meditation, breathing exercises and paying attention to each moment. It aims at increasing calmness and balance, which ultimately improves one's emotional well-being. In this practice it is required to be attentive to daily experiences and to cultivate the sense of acceptance and open-mindedness. Mindfulness also reduces stress, increases concentration and improves well-being of the practitioner.

In the Yoga Sutra, Patanjali discusses Prānayāma, however, he is not providing any breathing exercise. He is only telling us to become aware of our breath and its dynamics. There are four dynamics of breathing. In general, we are aware of three dynamics of breathing that are - ingoing breath, outgoing breath and the stillness of breath in between the two. There is also a fourth dynamic of Prāna that transcends the concept of any direction, because this Prāna is all pervading. We can become more and more aware of the fourth Prāna, when our Kundalini energy activates the higher chakras. It is also possible to integrate the three dynamics of breathing with the fourth Prāna. When this integration happens, we can feel the oneness with Spirit.

CHAPTER ELEVEN

VERSE 1-9

svapnovikalpāh

Dreaming level consists of passive imagination.

Dreams are assumed to have many purposes, although the exact reasons are not yet understood. Several theories explain that dreaming helps in balancing emotions, memory consolidation, in problem solving, and also can work as a type of subconscious desire fulfilment. The brain uses dreams for sorting through experiences and emotions from the waking level of consciousness.

Basically, what we see in dreams is our imagination running passively in the back of our mind. Dreams are not of the conscious mind. They are of the subconscious mind. With certain practices it is possible to engage the conscious mind with dreams. Then it is called Lucid dreaming. This helps us to fully recall what we see in dreams. While dreaming our brainwave frequency is usually at Alpha or Theta level. For dreaming, the body needs to be in a relaxed condition, such as sleeping. Daydreaming also happens when the body is in a relaxed and passive state and is associated with the Alpha level.

Passive Imagination is a type of limiting belief that wants to keep things the same. While a child grows up to become an adult, it gathers certain beliefs from its family and culture. Anything that is not in alignment with those beliefs is considered as not acceptable. These beliefs get attached to a person's identity in an unconscious way. It is a type of primitive safety mechanism which the body learns to avoid being isolated. In primitive cultures people learned to live and make compromises as a group to protect themselves from their wild surroundings. Even in contemporary culture the same safety mechanism is active, although may not be as much apparent.

These beliefs get passed down from generations to generations through a process of conscious or unconscious imitation. A child learns to become a copy of its parents by imitating the same beliefs and habits that the parents have. Although the child may acquire a different outward personality, the internal belief structure remains similar to the parents.

We can observe the mental chatter which is a form of imagination running passively in the subconscious mind. This chatter is reactions done by the internal limiting belief system. If the reactions are very strong it can drain people of their vitality and purpose. This is why many people live a safe but purposeless and monotonous life, living in a similar way that their parents lived their life. That way they can avoid the strong reactions in the subconscious mind. Patanjali compares this purposelessness to someone speaking words without any meaning.

VERSE 1-10

avivekomāyāsausuptam

During the peaceful state of deep sleep, one is unaware of Māyā.

Sleep is a need of the body. Without sleep the subconscious mind can become dysfunctional. During the waking hours the subconscious mind engages in various activities such as seeing, hearing, talking, eating, working, thinking etc. Due to paying attention to such activities the body uses its stored energy and becomes tired. Sleep is assisted by sleep hormones that certain glands produce. During sleep the body organs relax and it restores the energy levels. That is why we feel refreshed after a good sleep or nap.

If the mind is worried due to some issues, then that activates the survival mechanism of the body and it keeps us awake to ensure survival. On the other hand, sleeping too much makes a person lethargic and may not pay attention to important things.

Deep sleep or Delta level is connected to the purest form of consciousness, which we call God, Ishwara or Creator. The Delta level is a very peaceful state because there are minimum activities of the mind. The Creator is the one who creates the mind matrix called Māyā. Therefore, the Creator is above Māyā. Because of the deep connection of the Delta level with the Creator, when we are in deep sleep we are unaware of the matrix. The deep sleep state can be a doorway out of the matrix, if one can stay cognizant during such a state. With meditation also it is possible to achieve Delta level. If during meditation, we can achieve a completely peaceful and non-reactive state like Wu-Wei, it is what the Delta level is. Whenever I chant Nārāyana Nārāyana, it takes my consciousness swiftly to the Delta level. We can also use such trigger mechanisms like chants or mudras (hand postures) to activate specific levels of consciousness.

CHAPTER THIRTEEN

VERSE 1-11

tritayabhoktāvīreśah

One who is able to experience the Turiyā state at the three levels is a victorious overcomer.

There is a three step process for attaining the Turiyā or Samādhi state, which is mentioned in the Yoga Sutra. This process is the triad - Dhāranā, Dhyāna and Samādhi. In the VBT, there are about 112 Dhāranā provided. As mentioned previously, Dhāranā means Active Imagination. We can also call it visualization. As we practice these Dhāranās, they tend to gradually integrate into our daily life. At one point, these practices become spontaneous. Thus we can attain a profound state called Dhyāna. In the Yoga Sutra, Dhyāna is described as - tuning one's consciousness into a single vibrationless tone. It is what is known in Zen as the "sound of one hand clapping". Next, we can enter into Samādhi. I have realised that Samādhi also has two phases. First phase is like I-am-ness, which is Sabeeja Samādhi. The second phase is Oneness, which is Nirbeeja Samādhi.

With sufficient experience, we can directly reach Oneness without going through the triad process. Once we reach Oneness, we are above all limiting perceptions. We are even above our personality. It requires courage to go beyond our personality because it has attachments related to ego and memories. Once we are above our personality, we are the true Whole Self. That gives a feeling of joy and victory.

After we practice Oneness during waking hours, we will be practicing Oneness even during dreams and sleep, albeit unconsciously.

CHAPTER FOURTEEN

VERSE 1-12

vismayoyogabhūmikāh

The foundation of Yoga is the wonderful Self.

Yoga is the joyful overcoming of apparently rigid limitations constituted by the activities of mind-perceptions. I like to translate the word Yoga as Integration. It is the integration of the physical self with the Whole Self. Thus the Whole Self can be the goal as well as the foundation of Yoga. When we are integrated with the Whole Self, wonderful things start to happen. The experience of this integration is itself quite wonderful. The Whole Self is the greatest source of power. When this power is well directed, we can swiftly move towards any goal, alter realities and get divine assistance if required. Yoga Sutra mentions some special abilities called Siddhis which can be attained with the maturation of our Yoga practice. The discipline of Yoga can also help us achieve the four basic goals of human existence - Dharma, Artha, Kāma and Moksha. Essentially, with the practice of Yoga we become capable of overcoming any limiting beliefs, due to the integration with the Whole Self.

Yoga leads us to a high level of observation from where anything and everything can be observed, including the Self; a Self that is the self of all, i.e. the universal Self. The observer realises that even it is the Self and it can observe itself. Consciousness can observe consciousness and the universe at the same time. Such a high level of observation feels like vertigo to the subconscious mind. Hence, a mediocre person is uninterested in Yogic principles. However, the potential applications and benefits of attaining such a high level of consciousness are endless.

CHAPTER FIFTEEN

VERSE 1-13

icchāśaktirumākumārī

Will-power is surrendered to the gentle spirit.

The Whole Self is made of a substance that we can call as Spirit. Patanjali tells us to practice concentrating on Eka Tattva (one substance) in the Yoga Sutra. The Spirit is an all pervading substance. It exists in the physical plane, mental plane and beyond. At every moment there is the continuous transition happening between the beyond and the manifest, and vice versa. Science does not recognise the existence of Spirit yet, due to the lack of supporting evidence. It is said that Kirlian Photography has been able to capture some glimpses of the Spirit. Nevertheless, there are sufficient instances of events which make it difficult to completely deny the existence of Spirit. The words like Prāna, Chi etc. are closely related to Spirit. Patanjali calls it the "fourth Prāna".

I have a Master level certification in Reiki. There is an

intelligent energy that exists in the Universe which can be directed with human intention. By nature this energy is scalar, which means, it has momentum but no direction. With a skill like Reiki it is possible to direct this energy, by using intention to cause positive changes in our body, mind and environment. We can also use positive affirmations to upgrade our state of being. Affirmations carry the positive intentions to the Spirit.

The word Kumārī means "a little girl". The main characteristics of Spirit are that it is gentle, peaceful and non-judgmental - just like a little girl. When our conscious mind makes a connection to this Spirit, we feel more and more relaxed. The purpose of relaxing in this way is to move from Beta brainwave level to lower levels of Alpha, Theta and Delta. The will-power and desires that we express during waking hours are part of Beta level. When we surrender these emotions to the gentleness of Spirit we have a heart-centred perspective of everything.

VERSE 1-14

dŕśyaḿśarīram

The Spirit-body can be seen.

Let me illustrate a very simple Mandala as the following diagram:

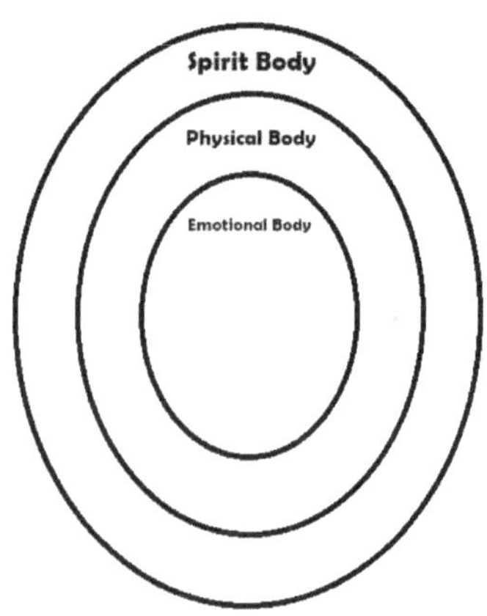

We can imagine ourselves as having three bodies - a physical body, an emotional body and a spirit body. The physical body is simply a follower. It either follows the emotional body or the spirit body. The emotional body mostly lives inside our physical body, though often it is also transmitting or receiving emotions with the environment and others. This body contains our emotions, identity, ego and memories. The drawback with the emotional body is that it believes in limitations. It can see something or someone as an obstacle. Its attitude is judgemental.

Through meditation it is easy to be in a state where it is possible to put aside the emotional body. Then the physical body comes directly in touch with the spirit body. The spirit body is the home of infinite possibilities. It is always in touch with the one intelligent substance of the universe. The attitude of the spirit body is loving and non-judgemental.

According to Patanjali, the key to overcoming limitations is to practice this detachment (Vairāgya) from the emotional body. Then the spirit body can take control and help resolve the limiting perceptions. Patanjali emphasises a lot on this practice.

By being more and more in touch with the Spirit body negative emotions are eliminated. Once we are able to balance our emotions, we become less reactive. When emotions are balanced Prāna energy is properly utilized in our body. Proper utilization of Prāna is the key to good health, vitality and longevity. The worst of the negative emotions is anger. In the Bhagavad Gita, Krishna says that the habit of being angry is our worst enemy. To be in a state of anger and vengefulness is quite common for ordinary humans. Anger depletes Prāna energy like nothing else. The root cause of anger is the ego which exists in the Emotional body. When we connect to the Spirit body we are able to forgive others, even if someone has harmed us a lot. This happens after connecting to the Spirit body because we realise our infinite potential, so there is no need to hold on to anger or resentment. Negative emotions may then be replaced by positive and elevated emotions.

CHAPTER SEVENTEEN

VERSE 1-15

hrdayeChittasamghattāddrśyasvāpadarśanam

When the Chitta rests in the heart, the visible world does not look serious.

In the Yoga Sutra it is mentioned that there are five types of Chitta Vritti, i.e. the activities of the subconscious mind. These are (1) Evident fact, (2) Imperfect idea, (3) Passive imagination, (4) Sleep and (5) Memory. While our attention is occupied in such activities, we are unable to recognise our true Self. The goal of the Dhāranās that we can practice from VBT is to reduce the activities of Chitta, so that we can realise Oneness or Turyā. Typically, we tend to take these activities seriously and thus think that our worldly identity is who we are. This type of thinking is called Māyā.

Pratyāhāra is a Yogic principle, which I like to translate as "letting go". It is about detaching from Samsāra and related desires. Samsāra consists of "opposites", i.e. polarity. If we contemplate both the opposites, then we realise that both are part of one and the same Samsāra. In fact, the literal meaning of Samsāra is "same in essence".

As we let go and detach from the seriousness of Māyā, then living in Samsāra becomes like playfulness. This playful attitude called Leelā is a more heart-centred way of living.

In Hinduism the concept of time is not linear, but circular. If we consider, for example, historical events, those are not just one time events. These events have previously happened countless times, and will continue to happen again and again. When we attach our emotions to such events, they appear to have happened only one time. There are parallel universes where those events are happening even at the present moment. Scientists have started recognizing the probability of parallel universes. Schrödinger's Cat experiment (a thought experiment) was carried out to determine whether parallel existences are possible or not, and it showed that such a probability does exist. At the quantum energy level, time is an illusion. So, only the present moment can be considered as real. The past and future are not so real and concrete.

Krishna tells Arjuna in the Bhagavad Gita to be Sthitapragnya, i.e. to live in the present moment. When our mind is not wandering into the past or future, then we have tapped into the elite state called Sthitapragnya. Everything happens only in the now. I have an intuitive understanding that the concept of parallel universe is represented by Rādhā, who was the lover of Krishna. Krishna too loved her dearly. Love is the doorway to the present moment. When someone asked Einstein to explain the Theory of Relativity in an easy way, he explained it in the following way: "When you sit near your lover for two hours you think it is only a minute, but when you sit on a hot stove for a minute you think it is two hours. That's relativity."

CHAPTER EIGHTEEN

VERSE 1-16

śuddhatattvasandhānādvāapaśuśaktih

By finding the pure essence, trapped energy is liberated.

There are five types of Kleshas or delusions mentioned in the Yoga Sutra. These are (1) avoidance of spiritual nature, (2) narcissism, (3) fondness, (4) competition and (5) idea of ownership. There is no direct way to control the delusions. The practice of Pratyāhāra and Turyā is the best way to reduce the impact of delusions. The delusions are like mud in a pond of water. When the water becomes still the mud settles to the bottom.

Thinking uses a lot of energy. Brain is a high energy consuming organ, which consumes about 20% of our body's energy, even though taking up about 2% of body weight. It has been observed in research that about 98 percent of thoughts that we have during the day are the same thoughts which we had the day before. Therefore, a lot of energy gets wasted in thinking redundant thoughts.

It is difficult to believe that the subconscious mind can be deluded, because we grow up and live with it. There are so many undercurrents in the subconscious mind which are created by previous experiences. When a person is born he/she is new to the world and does not have previous experiences. Gradually many conditionings develop in the subconscious mind due to our surroundings, i.e. because of interactions with the people and things around us. We lose connection with our original Self and choose to live an identity given to us by family and society. This identity may not be the right one for us. If we are brought up in a surrounding that is less deluded, then we possibly live the right type of identity; otherwise, it is not so. That is why it is important to go back and find our original Self, so that we can live our true choices, instead of living according to a world which is largely deluded.

The subconscious mind can have ideas that are not in flow with true wisdom. This type of idea has negative sentiments associated with it. If these ideas and negative sentiments are fed for too long, they can lead to disaster. It is born from ego states such as superiority complex or inferiority complex. These ego states can make a person blind to true wisdom, which causes the person to believe and propagate false, ambiguous or insufficient information as proper advice. To live a wholesome life, it is essential to cultivate true wisdom in our life. ·

When we connect to the Spirit, our thinking becomes less deluded, because Spirit is the pure substance which is associated with the Whole Self. This happens because our worldly identity gets superseded by the identity of the

Whole Self. The delusions are unable to get a hold on our thoughts because we are no more a worldly identity. The energy which was getting wasted due to delusional thinking is released and can be utilised for building a wholesome mind.

CHAPTER NINETEEN

VERSE 1-17

vitarkaātmajñānam

Self-realization eliminates argumentation.

People may argue for various reasons. They can have many types of perspectives and beliefs, which can lead to arguments. Disagreements or miscommunication can cause conflicts. Anger, frustration and tension can cause arguments. Opposing interests and desires can lead to disputes. Trying to have control or dominance in relationships or groups can result in confrontations. Economic or job related stress can contribute to conflicts. Differences in personality and temperaments can lead to quarrels. By recognising such factors it can help in managing and resolving arguments much more easily.

The meaning of Self-realization is to fully recognise and accept ourselves as we are. This process is generally associated with our spiritual, psychological, and philosophical areas. It is for recognising our authentic nature, hidden potential, and life purpose, and for aligning our thoughts, actions and emotions with that realisation. Self-realization is seen as associated with enlightenment, where an individual transcends the ego and identifies oneself with a universal consciousness. It fosters personal fulfilment and actualizing full potential. Self-realization basically is about gaining deep insight into ourselves, beyond societal identities for the purpose of living authentically.

During the process of self-realisation we realise that we are the universe, we are the all pervading consciousness and we are made of the pure substance called Spirit.

Due to the limited perceptions of the Chitta, many people tend to cling to their own point of view and believe that only their perspective is correct. They tend to argue and criticise others to try to prove their point. Patanjali tells us that a biased mindset becomes an obstacle to true understanding. However, there is another way to perceive things and it is called Pratyaya in the Yoga Sutra. Patanjali describes Pratyaya to be like a peaceful sunrise. Pratyaya is a type of intuition or direct understanding which can be attained after self-realisation. Pratyaya is beyond the activities of Chitta and the five senses. We can compare it with a submarine looking out through a periscope over the surrounding surface of water. Typically, our mind is like a submarine which is submerged in the activities of limiting perceptions and cannot see what is above those activities. Only when we attain the periscope of Pratyaya we are able to see what is beyond limiting perceptions. Attaining Pratyaya makes us more compassionate and empathetic towards others as well as us. Therefore, Pratyaya can eliminate all kinds of argumentation, criticism and self-criticism.

CHAPTER TWENTY

VERSE 1-18

lokānandahsamādhisukham

The gladness felt during Samādhi state attracts worldly happiness.

Happiness is understood to be the emotions such as the feelings of joy, contentment and pleasure. It is also about feeling fulfilment and contentment with life in general. Happiness increases by living a purposeful life and knowing that we have significance in society, while being deeply involved in activities of interest. It also means to have meaningful and supportive connections with our companions.

Ordinarily, we are in the habit of recalling past memories. Those memories may be personal, societal or historical. The memories are either of pain or of pleasure. When we recall a memory those experiences are replayed in our subconscious mind. It almost feels like our body is again experiencing those past events. The body has an innate mind of its own, which is called Chitta or subconscious mind. It functions mechanically based on impulses from the nervous system. When we recall a past experience, it triggers certain impulses in the brain and the nervous system. Thus the body mechanically assumes the memory to be a real experience. Due to the habit of recalling memories, when we remember unpleasant circumstances, we replay the whole situation again in the subconscious mind. This is the cause of sadness and tension.

Once in the Samādhi state, we let go of the attachments related to ego and memories. As a result, we reach an empowered position in which the memories are treated as inconsequential. According to Patanjali, the purpose of Samādhi is to reduce the impact of delusions. When our thinking is freed from delusions, we have a lot of energy that can be utilised to create favourable results. The mind remains calm because there is no conflict during Samādhi. In such a state, a spontaneous happiness is felt.

It is mentioned in the Yoga Sutra that how our mind perceives ourselves is what will be created in the world around us. When we are spontaneously feeling happy from inside, the outside world becomes favourable to us.

CHAPTER TWENTY-ONE

VERSE 1-19

śaktisandhāneśarīrotpattih

When Bhairava (Whole Self) finds the liberated energy and makes it bubbling with joy, the physical body rejuvenates itself.

Energy is defined as the ability to perform work or cause change. It may exist in several different forms, such as kinetic, potential, thermal, chemical, electrical, and nuclear. Energy may be transferred among objects and can be converted from one form to another, but it cannot be created or destroyed, according to a scientific principle known as the Conservation of Energy.

The consciousness of the Whole Self is Shiva and the liberated energy is Shakti. The energy that was trapped in delusions gets liberated once we are in contact with the pure Spirit, which is the substance of the Whole Self. When Shakti meets Shiva, who is the highest consciousness, this energy acts as a blessing. During this meeting we may hear the sound OM, which is the sound of creation. I have realised that the letter O represents divine masculine and M represents divine feminine. In the Yoga Sutra, OM is called Pranava, which means "all refreshing". Pranava has the quality of refreshing the mind and body.

The human body has an inherent healing ability. Fear and doubt are feelings which keep us from allowing this healing ability to work. Bhairava consciousness can convert the feelings of fear into tranquillity. Doubts are a type of self-criticism that gets eliminated when we attain Pratyaya. Ideally for healing to happen, we should be at the Theta brainwave level, where it is possible to alter our belief about the disease and replace it with a belief of sound health. At Theta level our brain behaves like the mind of a baby, so it believes whatever it is told to believe. Once we change the belief about a disease, the body's healing mechanism starts working to mitigate the health condition.

In the Yoga Sutra it is mentioned that the naval region is a place in which a symmetrical blueprint of the body is present. In Ayurveda also the stomach has a great significance. If the stomach is healthy then the whole body will be healthy. In VBT there is a Dhāranā to focus attention on the naval chakra to expand blissfulness of the mind. There is an obvious connection between our mind and body. It is not a coincidence that the words Health and Wholeness are synonymous.

CHAPTER TWENTY-TWO

VERSE 1-20

bhūtasandhānabhūtaprthaktvaviśvasamghattāh

When the source of all things (Bhairava) finds matter, then Bhairava can control and segregate the material world.

One of the names of Shiva is Bhūtnāth, which means Lord of the elements. Matter has many states such as solid, liquid, gaseous, plasma and intermediate states. There are several ways to classify matter, also including the periodic table used by science. Apart from earth, water, air and fire, space is also considered as an element in Hinduism. Space is considered to be the most "stable" element, because it is where all other elements exist. I like the chant Shivoham Shivoham, which I think means "I am that space where everything exists". There are multiple Dhāranās in VBT to focus on space. Because space is the lightest element, it has the least amount of activities. So, when we focus on space, the Chitta's activities are minimised and that helps us to reach lower brainwave frequencies. At Delta level we realise the transitory nature of everything.

Chitta or subconscious mind is the mind of matter (body). Chitta believes that it can "own" material things, even people. This belief is required because it is analogous to gravity holding objects to the ground. However, some people become greedy or controlling due to this belief. If we see on a larger scale, the Whole Self is the source of everything, hence is also owner of everything. When our vibration is close to that of the Whole Self, we are likely to attract more abundance. It would feel like the Whole Self is taking possession of its own house, and arranging it in an orderly manner.

When any thoughts of lack or limitation come, it is because of certain types of subconscious programming that we received during our lifetime. Such programming creates limiting beliefs about us. The Whole Self cannot have any lack or limitation, because everything belongs to the Whole Self. So, whenever any such thoughts come, we should remember our true self as the Whole Self. Thus if we don't give energy to such thoughts, those beliefs will wither away. Then we have the scope for having more empowered thoughts. It is said that our thoughts create our reality. Active imagination is a powerful tool for creating our own empowered reality. How we use our imagination determines how we feel and how we act. Therefore, by using our imagination wisely we can bring positive changes to our lives.

CHAPTER TWENTY-THREE

VERSE 1-21

śuddhavidyodayāccakreśatvasiddhih

As a result of the maturation of the Ishwara-self, rising of pure Vidyā happens that causes the opening/balancing of the chakras.

In the Yoga Sutra, Patanjali mentions Kriyā yoga. It is a type of Yoga that consists of three practices – (1) meditation, (2) understanding oneself, and (3) having faith in Ishwara. Patanjali also says that Ishwara is a Guru. The meaning of the word Guru is one who removes darkness by bringing light. When my Crown chakra was opened, I realised the presence of Ishwara as a divine light. When in contact with Ishwara, the spiritual world feels more real than the material world. To have faith in Ishwara ultimately means to understand that everything is and of Ishwara. As mentioned in the Yoga Sutra, one of the criteria for attaining proper Samādhi state is to have Bhakti (devotion) towards Ishwara. Bhakti means selfless love and selfless service. Because in Samādhi we need to leave behind our self-image, so it is important to be selfless first.

Ishwara as a personified creator is called Pūrūsha. If we consider in terms of Unified Field Theory of Quantum Physics, we will come to a conclusion that there is only one supreme person that exists in the world, subjectively. There is a Vedic Hymn called Pūrūsha Sūktam which also says the same. In the Bhagavad Gita, when Krishna showed his Universal form, it was observed that his form included all and everything. One of the names of Krishna is Adi Pūrūsha, which means Primordial Person.

Vidyā can be defined as habituated tendencies, conditioning or subconscious programming. There are two types of Vidyā - gross Vidyā and pure Vidyā. Gross Vidyā is something that we received from heredity (genes/DNA) and past/present life experiences. Pure Vidyā is what we develop during our spiritual advancement. As we make spiritual progress, gross Vidyā will be getting replaced by Pure Vidyā. There is a branch of science called Epigenetics, which states that certain diseases can be cured by altering genetic behaviour with the help of beliefs (including spiritual beliefs), without physical surgery or medicines. When a subconscious programming or belief is altered, the genes show a different behaviour.

Chakras are planes of existence. In the human body there are seven major nerve centres which are called the seven Chakras. The electromagnetic field around these nerve centres is denser than other regions of the body. If we could measure these electromagnetic fields with a highly sensitive instrument, they would look like wheels or

Chakras that appear like galaxies. In Yoga Sutra these are called seven-fold Pragna Loka (telepathic planes of existence). The word Pragna means telepathic communication. These planes of existence are doing telepathic communication with each other and the outside world. When we interact with other people, their Chakras do telepathic communication with our Chakras. These Chakras have the following associations:

Root Chakra (mūlādhāra) - Earth
Sacral Chakra (swādhisthāna) - Water
Naval Chakra (manipura) - Fire
Heart Chakra (anāhata) - Air
Throat Chakra (viśuddha) - Space/Sound
Third-eye Chakra (ājnā/āgyā) - Light/Consciousness
Crown Chakra (sahaśrāra) - Creator/Ishwara
We can consider these associations as planes of existence. If we look at it subjectively, these planes of existence are part of one and the same Pūrūsha. So, for example, even if our Sacral Chakra looks separate from the rivers, oceans, clouds, icebergs or the water in a jar, they are part of the same plane of existence. This subjective comprehension is called Samyama in the Yoga Sutra.

As we associate more and more with Ishwara, pure Vidyā rises that purifies our thinking and the planes of existence become well balanced.

CHAPTER TWENTY-FOUR

VERSE 1-22

mahāhradānusandhānānmantravīryānubhavah

By finding the great lake of oneness, the true potential of mantra is realised.

When we realise the subjectivity of the world through Samyama, the world appears to be more fluid, like one single lake. Due to this fluidity, any resistance that we have related to ego or self-image is dissolved. The sages of the past had told us that the world is "not real". What they mean is that everything in the world is subject to change. Even matter can transform from one state to another. In our body there is an ability called Neuroplasticity, which makes the body adapt based on circumstances. The great scientist Nikola Tesla used to say that when we think about the universe, we should think in terms of energy, frequency and vibration. This implies that to think about the world in terms of appearances is superficial.

There is a verse in Patanjali's Yoga Sutra which means - "The ultimate significance of microcosm and macrocosm is in the harnessing of it all". How is it possible to harness it? It is when our conscious mind (mann), subconscious mind (chitta) and superconscious mind (viveka) are aligned for the same purpose.

Mantras are powerful words or phrases repeated while doing meditation or praying. These are used to focus attention and for spiritual growth or relaxing the mind. Mantras are repeated to improve concentration during meditation, achieve a specific state of mind, and also to manifest a particular intention. Many also use mantras in their spiritual practices as a form of affirmation.

Before chanting mantras we should do Sankalpa, which is to set our intentions for the chanting. There may be many ways to do Sankalpa or Japa using sanctified items or a Mālā, but I don't want to discuss formalities in this book. I am only interested in discussing the underlying principles. According to Patanjali, while we do the chanting we should also keep in mind the meaning of the mantra. In VBT there is a Dharana which tells us to focus on the Heart Chakra while chanting mantras. The Heart Chakra has the widest electromagnetic field. Also, the Heart Chakra is the central Chakra with three Chakras above and three below. Therefore, if we chant a mantra while concentrating on the Heart Chakra the effect spreads evenly to all the Chakras. Those who do Mālā Japa, they would often bring their Mālā close to their heart, which helps to focus on the Heart Chakra. When we resonate with a mantra in the Heart Chakra, we are becoming one with the mantra. Heart Chakra is the chakra of silence, which is why it is called Anahata or unstruck. Any vibration, such as a mantra that we put into the Heart Chakra immediately becomes part of our being, as there is no resistance. Mantras are words of power. They can enable us to overcome any resistance, limitation and external influence. Our being that is the Whole Self is already very powerful. However, if our thinking remains entangled in limiting beliefs, then we cannot realise our true potential. The vibration of mantras invokes universal consciousness, which brings forth our true potential as the Whole Self.

In the next volume of my book (śāktopāya), which is all about mantras, I will explain more about mantras. I will share the meaning of popular mantras such as Shiva panchakshari mantra, Mahamrityunjay mantra, Navarna mantra etc. I have elaborated the meanings of these mantras based on intuition and personal experience.

In this volume, I want to share the meaning of one of the mantras, Gāyatri Mantra. The Gāyatri mantra is a gratitude mantra. It is about expressing unconditional gratitude towards Ishwara. When we express gratitude, we invite more abundance into our lives.

Gāyatri mantra with meaning:

OM, Bhūr Bhūvah Svah
Tat Savitūr Varenyam
Bhargo Devasya Dheemahi
Dhiyo Yo Nah Prachodayāt

OM, I invoke, That Luminous Purifying Benign Lord, who exists in all physical, mental and spirit worlds.

As I am established in thee, thus thee enable me to cast off impurities which gathered upon my intellect.
Truth dawns unto me and so I have known - Ah, I am fortunate!

Conclusion

It gives me the feeling of immense joy and satisfaction to share this book with the readers. I have stumbled upon and discovered many hidden secrets during my spiritual journey. At one point I realised that many of my realisations have ripencd and are ready to be presented in the form of a book. Life brings us situations that allow us to learn more about life and gain wisdom. Scriptures are another way for gaining wisdom because scriptures are based on the life experiences of spiritual seekers who came before us. While writing this book on Shiva Sutra I have realised that we as human beings have infinite potential, which we do not recognise if our mind is entangled in negative emotions and limiting perception. It is so important to accept our spiritual nature if we want full potential living. Many who realised their spiritual nature were able to excel in their pursued field of work. The deep seated beliefs that we hold about ourselves determine whether we will succeed in any undertaking. The main goal of the first method (Sāmbhavopāya) of Shiva Sutra is to overcome limiting beliefs. This is done by utilizing the principles of Yoga. I have had a long experience with understanding and working with the scripture Yoga Sutra of Patanjali. I have been able to integrate many of the teachings from the Yoga Sutra into my daily life. The most essential teaching of Yoga is to recognise ourselves as universal consciousness. This realization helps us to transition from ego-driven mindset to Pratyaya or intuition. Pratyaya is like a subtle song of the soul. Our soul gets wings when we attain Pratyaya. The spiritual achievements which are mentioned in the Yoga Sutra can be attained by means of Pratyaya and Samyama. The principle of Samyama is the heart of Yoga. It comes as a result of following the eight angas (organs) of Yoga. If we attain Samyama, we can realise ourselves to be as big as the universe or smaller than the smallest particle. Our perception of everything changes with Samyama, because Samyama is the undifferentiated consciousness, which is the Self of all.

I want to conclude with the following Vedic hymn:

Asatomā Sadgamaya
Tamasomā Jyotirgamaya
Mrityormā Amritam Gamaya

Let us move from deception towards clarity.
Let us move from limiting darkness of mind towards clear light.
Let us move from perpetual regeneration towards eternity.

Glossary

Sutra : Hint/thread

Patanjali : author of Yoga Sutra

Chitta : Subconscious mind

Mann : Conscious mind

Viveka : Superconscious mind

Māyā : Illusion

Leelā : Playfulness

Dhāranā : Active-imagination / visualisation

Turyā/Samādhi : Oneness

Zen : Japanese Buddhism

Klesha : Delusion

Pratyaya : Intuition

Bhakti : DevotionShakti : Liberated energy

Mantra : Repeatable words of power

Pūrūsha : Supreme person

Vidyā : Subconscious programming

Sankalpa : Setting intention

Pragna : Telepathy

VBT : Vigyana Bhairava Tantra

Author's Note

Understanding an ancient scripture and explaining it in such a way so that it may be accepted by the contemporary society required it to be illustrated with the help of information based on modern science. However, simply writing this book as a literary translation and with dry scientific explanations would have made it uninteresting to a lot of readers. That is why I have written this book with the primary objective of providing motivation to the readers. My book on Shiva Sutra has been written with my mind, heart and soul. The book includes broken down scientific analysis which fit into the content of the scripture. I have shared many of my personal experiences which I had while following the teachings of this scripture. I have explained only what I experienced while walking the path on my own. When I integrated the teachings of this scripture into my own life I experienced positive transformations. I was able to overcome negative emotions like anger, fear, worry and self-criticism. I have now been able to walk my life path with much more confidence, clarity and authenticity. In my book I have explained how anyone can overcome negative emotions and limiting beliefs, based on what I learned while applying the teachings from Shiva Sutra. I believe that every human being is capable of realising their full potential when they become authentic and free from distractions.

The Volume-I of Shiva Sutra is a small but power-packed book. It will train the readers how to develop their inherent spiritual abilities. They will be able to use their higher faculties of mind, such as intuition to take better and more productive decisions. The knowledge in this book can also help eliminate chronic issues like depression and anxiety, and may even assist in curing diseases. Such changes can be made possible if one can alter deep seated beliefs in the subconscious mind. In my book I have explained in detail how this can be done.

I believe that it is possible to have a positive outlook about everything regardless of the circumstances. When we can stay positive, we not only help ourselves but also the people around us. Positivity is the key to leadership. With my experience in my professional and personal life I have learned to deal with difficult situations. With my spiritual skills, I can now navigate such situations with much more ease, without feeling depleted. I believe that by reading my book many people can bring ease and positivity to their personal and professional lives.

Yoga Sutra of Patanjali - the fine fabric of integration

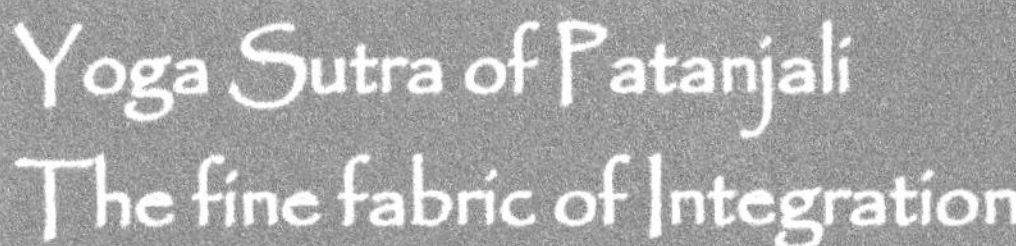

CONTRIBUTION

Apart from Shiva Sutra and Yoga Sutra, I am planning to do research on more Yoga related and Kashmiri Shaivism scriptures. If you enjoy my work and wish to add your generous contribution to my research, please use the following donation option. Thank you!

UPI (India): abhijit.bordoloi@icici

About The Author

Abhijit, an engineer by profession, lives in the city of joy Kolkata (Calcutta), India. He hails from the beautiful and mythologically significant town of Tezpur in Assam, a north-eastern state in India. Born and brought up in a religiously devout family, Abhijit received his education in science and engineering. Abhijit used to wonder how religion and science can fulfil each other, instead of being perceived as distinct or opposing disciplines. Abhijit has a Master level certification in Reiki and a long experience with Yoga. Shiva Sutra is Abhijit's first attempt at writing a book based on his own spiritual experiences. In his book, Abhijit has tried to blend spirituality, religion, science and motivational content in an enthralling way. The Shiva Sutra shows how to overcome limiting beliefs and unleash our full potential. Many spiritual secrets have been revealed in this book along with scientific explanations. Abhijit has a hobby of painting, and also enjoys music and sports.

Share your feedback:empirical.yoga@yahoo.com